RESTAURANT & BAR
MARKETING

THE NO BULLS#IT GUIDE
TO IMPROVING GUEST COUNTS

ERIK SHELLENBERGER

RESTAURANT & BAR MARKETING: THE NO BULLS#IT GUIDE TO IMPROVING GUEST COUNTS

Copyright © 2018 by Erik Shellenberger

Publishing services provided by  **Archangel Ink**

ISBN-13: 978-1-7241-3170-6

This book is dedicated to my friends and family who have stuck by me through it all. Mom and Dad, I love you. Amy Quint, you are the love of my life, and I'm honored to have a girl like you by my side.

CONTENTS

INTRODUCTION

Browsing Amazon's book section on bar and restaurant marketing, I see a consistent, glaring problem: outdated practices. Granted, this isn't the authors' fault; it's a fault of the industry. Still, these books are almost the only business resource available to a bar or restaurant owner today, and they all include:

- obsolete claims
- dated approaches to social media
- archaic marketing tactics like print media
- incorrect theories
- misleading use of online platforms
- inflated or just plain inaccurate stats

What was true yesterday is not necessarily true today. These factors may have been accurate at the time of publication, but by now they are the online equivalent of Harvest Gold appliances—dated.

I'm not immune to this problem. If you're reading this in 2020 or later, chances are this book is out of touch too, so I hope you'll pick up one of my newer books instead.

Looking over the online titles for the restaurant and bar marketing world, I thought, *Hell, I could do much better than this.* So I did.

How can I make such a bold claim? Because it's the story of my career success. I worked in both failing and successful bars and restaurants long enough to understand what they were doing right and wrong. Then I used that knowledge to run my own bar and restaurant marketing company successfully. That's the story I want to share with you.

A Lifetime of Learning

So there I was, a 35-year-old intern at a graphic/website design company, and not getting paid a single dollar for an entire year. I'd worked low-pay jobs before, but no-pay? That was new.

See, when I capped out the salary range for my job description in the automotive aftermarket, I knew it was time for a change, so I got out. My background was in the restaurant industry—I grew up in Park City, Utah as a snowboard bum, working at the ski resorts to score a free season pass during the day, and in restaurants at night to squeak by making minimum wage. That lifestyle was very tough to maintain and meant a dedication to a life of poverty. My mother owned the food and beverage department of one of the local resorts, so I had no trouble getting a job bussing tables for cash during my high school years.

I transitioned from bussing tables at a ski resort to washing dishes at a high-end restaurant on Main Street aimed at earning the tourist dollar. During these years, I worked in every conceivable position from server to bartender to manager to corporate marketing director. I even bartended at a goth dance club, of all things—a place called Area 51 in downtown Salt Lake City. I grew up as an angry punk rock kid with long hair, little direction, and very few options.

I attended Utah State University and the University of Utah but found out that college was just not my thing. I would rather make money than learn what I considered to be a bunch of meaningless bullshit. My parents were always there for me, but they encouraged me to support myself and pay my own way. I learned early on that I never wanted to be anyone's liability.

I spent winters in Park City and summers in Moab, Utah, where my father lived. As a product of divorced parents living in different parts of the state, I always had a place to crash if I needed it. Moab is considered the off-road capital of the world and an outdoor Mecca. That's where I got into off-road vehicles and opened my first business at 26 years old called 4-Wheel of Moab. I ran the place with one of my best friends of all time, Kelly Sheets. We fixed broken Jeeps and built up vehicles to be more capable off-road—real redneck shit.

Being full of piss and vinegar, I didn't really do my research. I didn't realize that Moab is very seasonal and couldn't support our business all year, so we had to close the shop in 2000, after 3 years of business.

Before long, I took a job as a salesman at the nation's biggest chain of off-road stores and moved back to Salt Lake City. I soon realized Utah just was not the place for me. I was born in California and moved to Utah as a kid; I wasn't Mormon and didn't really fit into what Utah wanted me to be. So, I transferred to Las Vegas. Vegas was awesome! Being single and a bit of a workaholic, I held my full-time day job and applied for a night job as a barback with plans to quickly move into a bartender position at the Palms Casino. I interviewed with three different people, including the director of food and beverage, which I thought was a bit excessive. *The director of F&B is interviewing barbacks?* Anyway, I got the job, which gave me the biggest high ever! *I'm going to be bartending at the fucking Palms in Vegas!* The very next day, my day job wanted to transfer me to Mesa, Arizona and made me an offer I couldn't refuse, so the Palms gig never happened.

I grew tired of corporate politics with the off-road chain, though. After my regional manager—who was an awesome guy and a great motivator—got replaced with an absolute prick, things took a turn for the worse. You know those guys who constantly got picked on in high school and now think it's their turn to ruin lives? Yeah, this was that guy. I was on my way out of the automotive aftermarket.

Finding a job in a completely new field with ZERO experience is damn near impossible unless you know someone, and that's how I became the 35-year-old non-paid intern.

Dodging a Bullet

After my year-long internship that felt like forever, I got a job as a corporate marketing director for a national chain of country music bars creating websites and making flyers. This was only possible because I knew the right people. Since I was still in the learning process, I accepted any extra work that got handed to me—without the additional salary, of course. When we needed a video made, I learn video editing. When we needed more difficult features added to our website, I learned that as well. Since I was already making the flyers, I was eventually handed the job of booking all of the country music concerts, including several national acts that you've heard of. I was also the social media guy, and back in those days social media actually reached quite a few people compared to today's numbers.

Run, Forrest, Run!

Unfortunately, this company turned out to be a one-man Ponzi scheme. My boss always had this mafioso persona about him, but I just thought he was acting tough. It turns out he was a former member of one of New York City's biggest crime families and was relocated to Arizona under the witness protection program! I smelled a rat after years of being with this company, so I got the hell outta there. A few years later, I ran into an article published online outing him and his shady background. He put away seventy mobsters in exchange for a lighter sentence and witness protection, more than almost anyone in history.

When I quit that job, I went to work in the Entertainment District of Scottsdale Arizona for one of the three companies that control all of the nightclubs along a fifty yard stretch in the most competitive zip code in the entire state of Arizona.

Shit Was Getting Real

I was the very first corporate employee at this company, a no-brainer to hire because I did the work of five different employees; I did everything myself. When the company failed to follow through on certain agreements, I went to work for one of the other three companies that control nightclubs on the same street. The nightclub environment in that district is about as cutthroat as it gets. Emotions and egos run high in this area and can cause people to do irrational things, even when sober. This area has thirteen bars and clubs in close proximity—sometimes a little too close for comfort.

I quickly realized the tactics we were using in the nightclub business were just being stolen from the competition—not because they were successful but simply because the other guys were using them! It became a vicious cycle: Company A is doing it, so company B starts doing it as well. Since company B is doing it, company C also starts doing it. And so on. It goes around and around in this bullshit circle. Everybody thought they had things figured out, but in reality, nobody knew what the hell they were doing. "Market Research" wasn't even a thing.

The standard marketing approach was boiled down to: Plan a theme party, make a flyer, put it on social media, and walk away. Done. The more events the club planned, the more flyers were made, and the more social media posts were uploaded—requiring more and more help to get these done. Costs went up, but profits didn't follow. Success or failure was hardly measured at all, if ever. Since the competition was using the same tactic, no one paid attention to measuring results; everyone was simply keeping up with each other. It was pointless! The events got so dumbed-down that it went from exclusive headlining event flyers with merit, to four theme parties per week that nobody cared about, to an unsuccessful happy hour that nobody went to.

The sea of flyers quickly became overwhelmingly spammy and mind-numbingly ineffective. The law of diminishing returns kicked in long before this, but since every operations manager was so fixated on what the competitor was doing, they never took the blinders off long enough to realize they were all losing participants in the same game. When Facebook's algorithm was constantly decreasing traffic and choking out the reach of business pages down to damn near nothing, hardly anyone noticed in the bar marketing community. I would bring up the need to pivot and evolve, showing Facebook's analytics as evidence. But everyone kind of shrugged and basically said, "Well, this is just how we do it." And that was that.

It was at this point, I did something unheard of.

So unheard of, in fact, that no one had ever thought to do it before. This idea was so left field and weird in the industry that I actually had a lot of pushback within my own company. Everyone I suggested this to brushed it off as meaningless busywork.

I know you're wondering: What was this approach that was completely alien to an entire marketing department?

I simply asked the public.

I started to poll the public and ask people what brought them in the door of one bar over the other. I asked people what online platforms they preferred. I asked them how their habits differed when they were in their hometown versus when they were on vacation. I asked them about the importance of word of mouth over using an online platform to find a place to eat or drink. I asked them what type of places they preferred to go to and why. Over the course of six years, I have asked every conceivable question about human nature when it comes to choosing bars and restaurants.

The results are the foundation of this book.

The poll results were quite interesting and often pointed to tactics *opposite* of what we'd been using. No longer were my thoughts just speculation; I was gathering actual data from real customers. I was using analytical numbers instead of assumptions. This was no longer a theory. When I brought this up to my bosses in several different locations, the data was met with: "Okay, we'll look into it." But rarely was anything done to change our marketing practices. Like I mentioned, egos were high, and this went against the grain of "how things had always been done."

I approached my boss and told him that by employing me they were wasting company money and that the entire marketing department was costing them more than it was making them. "That's the first time I've heard that one from an employee," he said. I quit that day.

I had started my company Bar Marketing Basics years back, but really hadn't taken it seriously until I saw the opportunity to go against the status quo. I was tired of being a sheep, so I started using the approach that actually works.

I have to say it's been one hell of a ride, and my business has become wildly successful using these tactics. I'm now living the life I designed. I was able to get out of the rat race, quit my 9 to 5 desk job, and start doing things my way, on my terms, on my time.

One More Thing

Before we dive in, I feel I should tell you… I write like I speak to my friends, not some stuffy-ass business guru writing you a "how to" book. I'm a firm believer in giving away every ounce of knowledge I've learned. I do this for one reason—because 99% of you will not follow all of these steps. Most of you will not have the time, so I'll still have a job regardless.

That said, if you don't mind gratuitous cuss words and car references, this book is for you. This is how you improve guest counts and get asses in seats. Now let's do this.

Chapter 1

GET OUT OF THE FISHBOWL AND INTO THE OCEAN

If I had to sum up the contents of this book into a single, coherent concept, it would be the fishbowl versus the ocean scenario. A fishbowl environment is made up of people who have heard of you before. Existing customers. People who have "opted-in," "liked," or "followed" you. This environment is represented by things like email lists, social media accounts, customer databases, and so forth. *Most continuing (and expensive) marketing efforts are geared toward getting more people into your particular fishbowl so you can continue to market directly to those people.*

Conversely, the ocean is made up of ALL consumers. People who have no idea you exist. People who are looking to branch out and try new places to eat and drink in their home city. People who have not opted in or liked anything you offer. The tourist economy is almost exclusively an ocean environment. It includes the person using Google or online reviews to find a business like yours.

In case you didn't catch it from the introduction, you need to understand that most restaurants and bars rely almost entirely on their fishbowls for marketing. They build databases and social media accounts without a care in the world for the consumer who is looking for a business like theirs outside their fishbowl. This is unfortunate, because …

The ocean—NOT the fishbowl—is where you improve guest counts.

How do I know this? It comes from the results of the polling I mentioned earlier. *This information comes from direct customer feedback.*

Since polling the public over the course of six years, one thing became apparent to me more than anything else. *Social media is given way too much credit for bringing people in the door of a bar or restaurant.*

I phrased this question in several different ways, to several different demographics, several different times; the results were always the same. Here are the big-picture results that my current approach is based on:

> **What brings a NEW customer to your door?**
>
> - **Word of Mouth - 65%**
> - **Online Review Platforms (Yelp, Google, Facebook reviews, TripAdvisor) - 20%**
> - **Google - 10%**
> - **Social Media - 4%**
> - **"Everything Else" - 1%**

We're all aware of the power of word of mouth. It's by far the most successful tool for driving people in the door. The problem is, we marketing people are powerless to affect this. Word of mouth is influenced by operations, not marketing. Word of mouth is based on past experiences of friends, family, and even strangers. It's operations—*NOT the marketing department*—that turn a one-time customer into a regular. Sure, the marketing department can post a new and exciting menu item on Instagram to bring that person back in the door, but if their first experience wasn't a good one, chances are they're not coming back—no matter how good that new taco looks.

Google and online reviews are particularly important and powerful tools if you're catering to the tourist market. When it comes to dining habits, human nature differs greatly, depending on if the person is in their hometown—a familiar environment—versus out of town in unfamiliar territory. Out-of-towners tend to ask a local or a hotel concierge when looking for the best place to grab a bite. This is followed by using an online review platform like Yelp or TripAdvisor, followed by a simple Google search.

The effectiveness of social media to bring NEW people in the door is shockingly low, but if you think about it, it's common sense. People can't like or follow your restaurant if they've never heard of you.

So, what about that other 1% of people who find your restaurant or bar from the "everything else" source? What the hell is that supposed to mean? This is all of these weird phone apps that no one's ever heard of, obscure online resources and tech tools that aren't quite there yet. With the exception of apps based on existing online platforms like Yelp, no phone app has broken into the restaurant and bar industry enough to move the needle.

Believe me, I tried it.

I spent a ridiculous amount of time and money building an app that basically gave people free food in their geographic location, based on criteria they designated in the app. It turns out, people will not give up their home screen real estate even for a free meal. Getting someone to download an app in the first place remains the biggest barrier to the success of apps. Human nature tells people that apps slow down their phone and drain their battery. Whether it's true or not, this is the belief. Phone apps in the restaurant or bar field are just screwed.

The lure of the shiny new app for your business can be strong, but more often than not they are a waste of your time and money.

The biggest secret to effective marketing is NOT copying what everyone else is doing. Effective marketing is about trying to figure out which path human nature will take the customer down and meeting them there. Trying to go against the grain of human nature requires monumental shifts in behavior, like teaching people to buy products over the Internet instead of walking into a physical store. If you're trying to go against human nature to promote a theme party that doesn't make sense, for example, you're doing it wrong.

Human nature is why people find new restaurants to visit from these three main sources: word of mouth, review sites, and Google, NOT social media. When doing a "right here, right now" search, these are the go-to tools people use.

Putting Social Media Reach in Context

I asked consumers: "How influential are a bar or restaurant's social media posts to the frequency of your visits?"

Here's what they said:

- 26% see the posts but don't pay much attention[1]
- 22% do not make dining or drinking decisions based on social media posts
- 15% report social media posts have zero effect on their visits
- 12% don't even follow their favorite places on social media
- 9% only pay attention to special events advertised on social media
- 2% answered "other" (we'll assume this is a yes, they use social media to find restaurants)
- The percentage of people who make decisions about where to go exclusively based on social media posts? **14%!**

So to sum this up: about 84% of responders say that social media more or less does not affect their visits one way or another.

Think of your social media reach like this: Total up your Facebook and Instagram likes and followers. That is the MAXIMUM number of people who could potentially see your marketing message. The

---

1   Keep in mind, this is over the course of six years, so back in the day these posts would have been a lot more visible than in 2018.

reality of Facebook today is that about 1% of your followers will *actually* see your posts. So, best-case scenario for an average restaurant with 5,000 followers combined is that about half of them will potentially see your message (mostly through Instagram). Out of the 2,500 potentials, about 1% of them will take action. How much money is it worth to you to bring 25 people in the door? That is the question you must ask yourself.

Note that paying for social media ads is not included in this equation. That's a different topic I'll get into later. Yes, there are certain techniques that operate outside of this scenario, but I'm going to concentrate on the majority of restaurants and bars that do not use those techniques correctly, or at all.

Don't get me wrong. I love social media.

This may seem like I'm bashing the effectiveness of social media. Quite the contrary—I love the power of social media, and I'm very active on Facebook and Instagram myself. It's when businesses ignore the other half of the equation that my Common Sense Detector kicks in.

Check out this graphic. It shows what happened to our traffic in December of 2017. Organic reach dropped off to almost nothing after the algorithm changed, and from that point forward, your Facebook posts were seen by an all-time low number of your followers.

Everyone who markets a business through a Facebook page experienced this sharp decline in traffic. I wrote a blog post on this subject a few months prior to warn my clients that this was coming. It was no secret to people who research stuff like this.

What this means is that Facebook is, now more than ever, a "pay to play" environment. Organic reach is pretty much a thing of the past on Facebook. I couldn't remember seeing many of the bars and restaurants that I follow come up in my feed, so one day I did a little experiment. I checked my "pages feed" on my personal account and noticed that I follow 800+ businesses on Facebook. I started to scroll back in time to count the number of their posts that were visible to me as a consumer and someone who "likes" their page. I scrolled, and scrolled, and scrolled until my index finger had enough. I went back through a two week period and tallied up the number of organic posts that I saw. The grand total was … ZERO. I did not see one single post from a restaurant or bar that I had signed up to see! The only exception was the sponsored posts, which the business had paid for to be among the visible posts in my feed.

"Yes, BUT I can measure my impression numbers, and people are still seeing my posts somehow," you say. True. Sort of. Not everyone's settings are the same, and not everyone sees the same things in their feed. I was mentioning this to a client. He logged into his account, and within minutes he found a non-sponsored organic post from a bar that he "liked." We checked my settings against his and couldn't find any differences, but his phone was showing different content than mine was. It seems the default settings are quite a bit more like the ones on my account. I have tried this same challenge dozens of times since, and the results are usually the same as my original experiment. The takeaway is: Almost nobody sees a business's non-sponsored posts.

What do impressions really mean?

Impressions are the number of times your post cruises by on someone's screen with the potential of them seeing it. Here is a screenshot of a recent ad campaign regarding the fishbowl-versus-ocean concept. Check out how many paid impressions I got; compare that number to the organic impressions. Keep in mind that paid reach will also cause your organic reach to increase. Without paid reach, my posts on this page usually get double-digit impressions only. I am no longer active with this business page as a result.

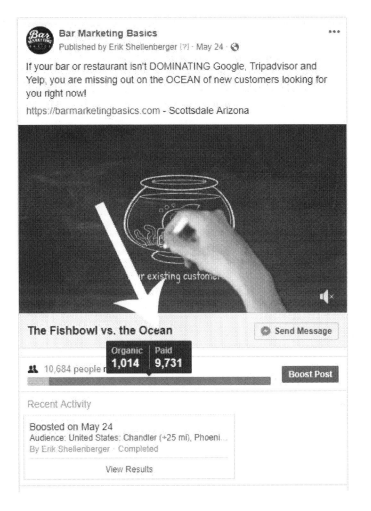

The other issue I have with impressions is that an "impression" doesn't necessarily mean a potential customer or even a human being has spotted your post; many of these impressions are seen by bots. "Bots" are basically computers dedicated to collecting data or completing tasks way quicker than people can. In this case, bots also crawl Facebook business pages and rack up the impression numbers. If you do the math on impression versus interaction, it doesn't make sense. If 5,000 people see your post but you get two likes and no comments or shares, real people aren't really seeing them. And while we're on the subject, let's be honest: the number of likes and shares you usually get are from the staff members whose job it is to promote your content.

Can you see now why the fishbowl is not the most efficient and cost-effective use of your resources?

Adapt and Pivot

When I interview a potential client, I'll always ask them the same thing. We review their marketing tactics, which are a carbon copy of everyone else's. We look at their social media posts and impressions, and the conversation goes something like this:

Me: Your posts aren't getting much interaction. You have a few likes here and there but almost no comments or shares.

Them: Yeah, I know. It's been like that since we opened.

Me: So what have you done to change up your approach?

Them: Not really sure what you mean. Like how?

Me: Your photos are shitty cell phone pictures. Your burger looks like dog food. Your text is always brief and boring like, "Come join us for happy hour." It's always the same subject matter. We both know this isn't effective, so what have you tried differently?

Them: Well, nothing really.

Me: So why do you continue doing something that is obviously failing?

Them: That's just what I was told to do, I guess.

Copy, paste. Rinse, repeat. Crap in, crap out. It's always the same conversation! For some reason, human nature traps us into believing that since you were told, "That's just how it's done," you aren't free to try your own approach. If I kept hitting my finger with the hammer, I would certainly make it a point to pay more attention to my hammering and learn better techniques.

Why Hiring "Social Media Experts" Is Not the Answer

You might be trying to skirt around this social media issue by thinking if you just pay an expert, you can get the results you want. Stop it. That doesn't work either. In fact, you'll be losing even *more* money.

If I hear one more goddamn social media manager pitch, I swear I'm going to lose my mind. People who want to "manage your social media accounts" rarely, if ever, focus on *your* success. They focus on theirs. They don't care about bringing people in the door; they care about "posting every other day with a photo or video post and writing keyword-rich text to accompany the posts." Mindless bullshit! What's worse is that these people often charge thousands of dollars per month for this service. I just saw a proposal for a small restaurant: For five posts per week—using the restaurant's existing content, mind you—they wanted $3,500 a month! The odds of getting that money back from an investment like this is not mathematically possible.

Let's do the math. Take a restaurant with roughly 5,000 Facebook followers and 5,000 Instagram followers—just to keep nice round numbers. A percentage of them are going to be the same person following this restaurant on both platforms; let's say a conservative 20%. When you remove the double-dipping from one of the platforms, that leaves roughly 9,000 followers. Of these followers, 84% of the people polled said they would not walk in the door based on this approach, so that leaves 1,440. If we apply the 1% rule of advertising—that 1% of these people will take action based on this approach—that means 14 people will potentially walk in the door. Here's the tricky part: Do we base this on a per-post average? The law of diminishing returns will kick in way before this is a reality. Do we base this off a weekly average? Monthly? Annually? Also, the quality of the posts greatly affects this number. No one will ever really know this number.

So now you've got your social media management company charging this client $3,500 a month to post five times a week. Let's use the best possible scenario; let's assume they're stellar. They create WAY above-average posts that bring those 14 people in the door per DAY. Hell, I'll even throw in the weekends when they aren't posting. That's 420 people over the course of a 30-day month. With a per-person average of $15 in the case of this client, that would bring $6,300 in additional revenue through the door. Not bad! BUT the average restaurant's profit margin is about 3–5%, topping out on the high end at 15%. So again, let's use the best-case scenario and say these guys are killing it and bringing 15% profit to the bottom line. So the client keeps 15% of that $6,300 they just brought in the door, which is $954.

It just cost you $3,500 to make $954!

Again, this example is in a perfect world. This is the *best-case scenario*, which is completely unrealistic. Do we use that number as a benchmark and pay the social media guys anything under that? No! You accept that the whole model doesn't serve your goals.

To be fair, social media success isn't based on each post performing well. It's about building brand recognition, getting your brand in front of someone's face over and over. And that is not at all measurable, which is why I don't like this model.

Stop relying on your social media fishbowl to make you money. And don't think that hiring a social media expert is the answer.

This also throws the "social" part of social media out the window. These posts are supposed to create conversations, not act as a one-way street. God forbid someone actually asks a question by commenting on one of your posts. Who's going to be there to answer it? Chances are, a "social media expert" will not. If someone comments: "Great post. What time is your happy hour?" and the information isn't easily accessible via a Google search, there's a good chance the potential customer's question will go unanswered. BUT your server who wants to make a few extra bucks to run your social accounts can address the customer's question.

Do NOT spend a lot of time or money on organic social media posting. If you have a simple approach, then get a server to do this for you.

The "Groupon" Model

I almost hesitated to include this, but since you have questions, I've got answers. What's wrong with the Groupon model? I have a perfect analogy for you:

> There was a restaurant called Saddle Ranch here in Scottsdale a while back. It was owned by the same guy who has the famous location on Sunset in Hollywood. It was a very cool, trendy place. When you sat down to eat, the hostess would say, "The owner would like to buy your first round of drinks on the house." You'd get a free round! Call drinks, premium, anything you wanted was included. It was a great value proposition and made you feel like you were getting away with something. People would go there specifically because they knew this was

coming, then they would proceed to drop $400 on dinner for the group. Not a bad model.

Sooner or later, when popularity dropped off and it wasn't the cool place to be anymore, the degenerate drinking public that Scottsdale is so famous for would go in, grab the free drink, and bail to the next bar. It wasn't encouraged but definitely allowed by the policy.

This is what Groupon has become. Groupon was a great idea when it started. It allows people to pay for only about 50% instead of the full price. The house would kick down another 25% for this privilege, so the restaurant ended up giving a 75% discount to a party that was otherwise willing and able to pay full price! The idea was that Groupon would turn people on to a new restaurant they didn't know existed in exchange for a huge discount. In reality, this was rarely the case. It was the return customers taking advantage of the discount.

Other online platforms started copying this model in droves, but it was nothing new; they were almost identical. I must have heard the same pitch once a week in my days as a corporate marketing director. Groupon has since changed its model because they were quickly becoming a name on par with the dreaded Y-E-L-P. They now register the customer's debit card, and when the customer makes a purchase at your restaurant, they get a discount on the back end; the server doesn't even know they are a Groupon user.

This is a good thing. Groupon users are notoriously shitty tippers and the first to complain on online review sites. They are people who do not manage their expectations and go to a place simply because there is a deal. This is a recipe for disaster. Groupon brings out the bottom-feeders, the deal-seekers. In the end, it's detrimental to your brand. Like a sinking ship, you can tell the failing businesses when the Groupon deals start to surface.

Making Your Money Count

Most people can wrap their heads around social media: Uploading a photo, writing a caption, and hitting "post." The results are instantly visible. When you ask the average bar or restaurant manager how to get to the top of the Google search results, you can almost hear their head imploding. This is straight-up voodoo for almost everyone out there.

Google isn't fun and interactive like social media. You can't connect with friends on Google searches. There aren't funny cat videos. But guess what?

It will *make you money.*

There's a huge world out there looking for what you offer, but if they don't know you exist, you're missing a *huge* piece of the puzzle. Start increasing your guest counts by getting your head out of the fishbowl and into the ocean!

Chapter 2
KEEP YOUR EYE ON YELP

Inevitably, when I bring up Yelp to a prospective client, the first words out of their mouth are "Fuck Yelp!" I get it, Yelp is a four-letter word for almost every bar or restaurant owner because the platform has positioned itself as a moderator between the restaurant and the pissed-off one-star reviewer whose account of what happened during his visit is usually FAR from the truth. Yelp reviewers are prone to gross exaggeration.

Don't get me wrong, Yelp is a great tool. It just tends to attract whiners.

The Yelp algorithm "flags" and removes some reviews but allows others. When these obviously exaggerated negative reviews get brought to the attention of Yelp employees, they just say, "Sorry, man, it's not my call. It's the algorithm." This is unfortunate, but hopefully not permanent. When blockchain technology (keep your eye on Synchrolife.org) solves all of this, Yelp will be a thing of the past. Until then, it's something we all have to deal with.

Unfortunately (or not), the public uses Yelp A LOT. In my research, Google has just passed Yelp as the most used online review site for mobile devices, but Yelp still has a big footprint in helping consumers make decisions about where to eat or drink. For some reason, girls tend to lean Yelp, and guys tend to lean Google. I have no idea why. Yelp is supposed to be an unbiased place for people to leave reviews based on actual experiences with a business. It has somehow morphed into a platform for complainers to bitch about anything and everything. Yelp can get real petty real quick. If you compare the overall star rating on Yelp to Google for a particular business, Google will almost always be higher.

Don't Let the Haters Get You Down

The worst environment that brings the complainers out of the woodwork is the dance club scene. Now, I'm too old for that shit—but even when I was in the correct age bracket, it wasn't my thing, so I don't really understand the constant negativity. But, MAN, does it get deep! This is the perfect storm of people who are barely of legal drinking age, can't afford to be there in the first place, and have no idea how to conduct themselves in public unsupervised. The entitled-little-bastard element is more prevalent here than in any business I've seen in an online review platform. There are two types of constant complaints stemming from these clubs, and it seems the more popular the place is, the worse the complaining gets.

Bottle service and the door bear the brunt of the complaints.

The door of any bar or club is where the issues are, but it's at its worst at dance clubs. Read the reviews for any trendy club—ANY club— and you will see one constant falsehood of racism at the door. Clubs have dress codes and do not let people in who are overly intoxicated. If these small problems are let in the door, they usually become huge problems later. In my experience, they are enforced equally between all races, but inevitably, you will get the guy who happens to be (insert race here), who will say it's because the doorman is racist. I've seen this from every conceivable race directed at the door staff—who are of every conceivable race as well. People believe what they want to believe; they're quick to disregard facts when they don't align with the story they're telling themselves. The poor doorman gets yelled at and receives the majority of the potentially drunk customer's rage, despite the fact he's the only sober person in the equation and is making minimum wage.

For the remainder of the people who make it in the door, bottle service is the next source of online complaints. Bottle service is the fine art of selling a $40 bottle of champagne to a customer for $1,000. Throw in the right DJ and enough pretty women to go around, and this makes sense to some. If you're one of the people at the dance club who actually dances and brings sand to this beach, these tables become $1,000 purse storage facilities. But no matter. For both the people who can afford it and the people who are in way over their heads, they expect service to match the price tag. In certain states like Arizona, the bottles have locks that must be removed by the server before pouring drinks. More times than not, these servers will have more tables than time. Sometimes they simply don't care about good service. Either way, if you're spending $1,000 on a bottle of cheap champagne and have two hours before last call, you need to drink quickly! When the bottle girl disappears—along with the guy's chances for a buzz staring him in the face without being able to indulge—his blood pressure tends to rise quickly. The clubs are a weird environment for a weird type of consumer, so we can't really apply this to normal life.

Yelp Can Do Serious Damage

Yelp can do a lot of damage to a new business while they hide behind the algorithm. I recently had a client open a new location and didn't start out with a great overall review rating. They were hovering around the 2.5-star range, and while they were a bit unprepared for the grand opening, they didn't deserve this. If you scroll way to the bottom of the reviews, there is a gray link that says, "Other reviews that are not currently recommended." These are the reviews that have been flagged and removed—most likely by this algorithm. I analyzed the hidden reviews and found that my client had nine negative reviews removed and 155 positives removed! Yes, 155!

I met with management to discuss the reviews, and they recognized several of the reviewers as legitimate customers who had a great time and wrote an authentic review based on their experience. Others were regulars at their other location; these were also legit reviewers. Obviously, this algorithm is severely flawed, and it impacted this business in a negative way. Most people reading this have likely had a similar experience with Yelp. Hence, the universal hatred of the platform.

This is usually the point at which people say, "Yeah, they want you to pay them in order to increase your review ratings." In Yelp's defense, this is not true in my experience. The Scottsdale Yelp office is across the street from several of the corporate offices I've worked at in the past, and I've had multiple meetings with them over the years. After a meeting where they tried to sell me advertising, I grabbed one of the guys while everyone else was out of earshot and said, "Okay, it's just you and me. We both know you can affect these ratings, so help a guy out. What's it going to take? I'll buy your advertising if you can take care of this negativity in our ratings." He said, "Honestly, there's nothing we can do. If you need to pass because of this, I'll have to let you." When I pressed him a bit more, he explained that his department isn't even close to the review removal guys. In the end, we bought the advertising. Nothing changed with our star ratings—if anything, they continued to go down. We eventually canceled.

So, on the subject of buying advertising from Yelp: Don't. Even if the rabid pit bulls they call salesmen call you relentlessly and give you the hard sell, don't do it. These people are far more ruthless than bill collectors and will drive you out of your mind until you finally crack because of the sheer pressure they can dish out. They remind me of timeshare salespeople. The only sales teams that are this aggressive are the ones with a worthless product to try and sling—in my humble personal opinion, of course.

I have done plenty of research on the subject, trying to actually find the value in what Yelp offers, but so far I haven't found it. I pulled analytics from before buying Yelp advertising and after, using several measurable methods that all referenced an investment of $700–$1,000 a month that failed to move the needle—and this includes several different locations and concepts. That's a sizeable investment with no return. People will find you on Yelp whether you buy advertising or not, no matter what the Yelp salesperson tells you.

Yelp offers several products; one of them is the Sponsored Listing, which can put your profile at the top of the search results surrounded by a blue box that says "Ad." Just like Sponsored Google results, human nature tells us to disregard those completely and go directly to the first organic result.

I used to dread these sales calls from Yelp because I'm the contact number on file for a lot of businesses. Now I love going head to head with them to see who can out-research the other guy. They are taught to have the rebuttal cards handy and know the correct way to handle any pushback. Unfortunately for them, I know every rebuttal for every rebuttal—and mine are backed by personal experience and research. I once prefaced a sales call by saying, "There's absolutely no way I'm going to buy from you. But if you'd like to discuss this anyway, I'm all ears." I let her go on and on, and we debated for over an hour. At the end of the call, she asked for the sale. I said I was pretty clear about that with my first sentence, but I appreciated the healthy debate. Bye, Felicia.

Bottom line? Save your money and put it into getting found on Google! You'll be much better off.

Respond to EVERY Online Review—Good and Bad

Now that we've covered the Yelp don'ts, let's go over the Yelp do's. *Do* respond to every online review you receive. Facebook, TripAdvisor, Yelp, and Google—respond to ALL reviews, good and bad, in a timely manner. In sickness and in health. Don't get in the habit of "putting out fires" on Yelp and ignoring the positives. Of course, you need to fix the bad reviews and get that customer back if at all possible. But get in the habit of thanking your fans for their positive feedback! Do this because not only is it the right thing to do for someone who is helping your business by offering positive feedback, but also because chances are, your competition isn't doing this either.

One of the easiest ways to keep up with this is to make sure your business's reviews are sent to your phone so you can respond immediately. You should try to respond within a 24-hour window. Flag any review that is flaggable, and take your online reputation seriously. If you don't have time, get a trusted employee to do it for you. If this isn't possible, or if their responses sound like they're written by a poorly trained robot, I'll do it for you. This is one of the services I provide for my clients. And trust me, there is an art to saying the same thing 100 times in 100 different ways.

Include these elements in your responses:

- Call the customer by name if possible.
- Issue them a thank you or an apology, depending on what the situation calls for.
- Invite them back in.
- Mention something specific to their review; don't just write a generic statement.
- Always sign your responses with your name, title, contact email, and phone number.
- For negative reviews, if it's warranted, offer to buy them their next meal on the house if they are open to another return visit. Contrary to what you might think, offering free meals publicly will NOT promote more negative reviews in hopes of another free meal; it never happens.

Do not hesitate to leave your cell number. If someone does reach out to you, it will go directly to you and not to the hostess. Leaving the main restaurant phone number will cause even more confusion and result in your upset customer going straight to the irate zone.

Don't worry—people will not blow up your phone.

Trust me, my cell number is on the review responses for tens of thousands of reviews, and I hardly ever get any calls. I get a few texts per month from customers of the clubs I worked with for two reasons: The people who want to spend thousands of dollars at the club for overpriced champagne and can't get the VIP host to answer his phone (seriously), and the people who were just about to leave a scathing 1-star review on Yelp but saw my phone number and decided to reach out instead. I'm able to save the company thousands of dollars per month by simply being personally accessible.

Whatever you do, do NOT copy and paste responses! This is the only thing worse than not responding at all. A few more things to consider:

- Don't use words like "strive." *Of course you strive to provide the best experience possible!* This is a meaningless statement.

- If your staff dropped the ball, own it and apologize. Obviously, never make excuses you can't back up.

- Remember you're not just responding to the author of the review, you're responding to the public. Always respond publicly, never in a private message. Without responses, the public is reading a one-sided conversation and taking in inaccurate or misleading statements quite often.

Consider the following:

Here is a common 1-star review: "Don't go here. After getting my bill I noticed that drinks are $15! Never again. Way overpriced!" You can then respond in a very professional manner with something like: "Thank you, Mr. Person, for your review. However, you were drinking double Ketel tonics, which is our most expensive drink. Our drinks start at $6 and go up from there. Thanks for your review!" The public reading this review and potentially about to stop in, won't think you sell well vodka singles for $15. They also know you're not an emotional wreck like the reviewer.

Your fans deserve a response as well.

Even if you have a very positive overall star rating, you still need to respond to your reviews. For example, a client of mine with a breakfast restaurant has a very strong 4.5-star rating on Yelp. The biggest complaint is that there is too long of a wait to be seated. They are on a waiting list during all peak times; for a breakfast restaurant, this means pretty much at all times. So, prospective customers reading the Yelp reviews would see these complaints back to back. Even though customers left a 5-star rating, they mentioned it took an hour to get seated.

This could be a pretty huge turnoff to a customer without a lot of time to spend.

But imagine if these reviews showed responses like: "Thank you for the great review. Keep in mind, if you call our hostesses about 30 minutes prior to your visit, we'll put your name on the list so you don't have to wait at all!"

Looks a lot more inviting, doesn't it? You provided information customers would never have known without a response to the positive review.

What if you get a negative review that just isn't true? Yelp says publicly they won't get in the middle of these disputes. In other words, false accounts of a visit are totally fair game on Yelp. You can flag any review at any time from your end, but the only ones that actually get removed are those that violate terms and conditions. These are your options for asking to have a Yelp review removed:

- it was posted by someone affiliated with the business
- it was posted by a competitor or ex-employee
- it contains threats, lewdness, or hate speech
- it doesn't describe a personal consumer experience
- it violates Yelp's privacy standards
- it contains promotional material
- it's for the wrong business

If it's just plain bullshit and didn't happen like the reviewer described, Yelp will always side with the consumer.

The Most Hilarious Review I've Ever Seen on Yelp

Sorry, Millennials, but you take the cake for the funniest and most entitled Yelp reviews of all time. We've all seen the reviews that start out "If I could leave negative stars, I would!" I saw one for a club that admittedly didn't have great reviews, but they were in the process of hiring better bartenders and actively trying to improve.

The reviewer's avatar was a picture of a very attractive younger girl who apparently had gotten used to having things handed to her in life. I'm paraphrasing her review, but it went something like this: She went into the loud club on a busy weekend night, and the bar was three or four deep. She asked what they had on special. (Rule #1 of a bar: don't do this!) She admitted she didn't hear what the bartender said but heard something was on special for $4 that night. So she just said she'd have a vodka soda. She paid cash, and he gave her $3 change for her $10 bill. At this point, she completely lost her shit and assumed he was "taking" a $3 tip. She said, "I thought you said drinks were $4?!" He said, "No, you asked what was on special, and I told you Captain Morgan was our sponsored drink of the night. But you ordered a vodka soda, which is $7." She absolutely freaked the hell out at this point and demanded to see the manager, who was probably running around doing five things at once. But in her words, he was, "Too busy to help me."

Keep in mind the poor bartender was still four deep with people he was trying to serve. He offered to buy her another drink for the hassle, which was more than most bars would have done. He poured the second drink when she finished the first one, handed it to her, and apologized again. She waited for a second, and when he moved on to the next in line, she flipped out on him again and accused him of stealing from the bar. He gave a confused look at this girl yelling, "I watched you pour me this drink that you said you'd buy me, and I CLEARLY did not see you open your wallet and pay for it. You basically stole this from the bar! Where is your manager?"

At this point, I think the guy had enough and moved on with his line of people backing up. The reviewer was completely outraged and wanted to get the poor guy fired—just for doing his job.

This is what happens when you don't know how to operate in the real world. Some people should stick to frat parties until they are 30.

The girl's name was actually Felicia.

Chapter 3
DON'T FORGET ABOUT TRIPADVISOR

If you own a bar or restaurant in a tourist economy outside the United States, TripAdvisor should be your best friend. You should be ranking high on all of their lists. And, as we discussed in the previous chapter, you should respond to all of these reviews. When you are the one business responding to your reviews, since no one else takes the time to do so, it paints you in a very good light. You can also correct false information like I mentioned in the chapter on Yelp. TripAdvisor works a lot like Google: the more complete your profile, the better you'll rank. Fill out every field possible and upload every photo you can that accurately represents your business.

On a recent trip to Aruba, I saw the power of TripAdvisor firsthand. Aruba has a string of hotels lined up along one section of beach, and directly inland across the street with all of the restaurants aimed at separating the tourists from their money. It was what you might expect: boring concepts with trendy-sounding names and average menus. My girlfriend and I hit a few of these due to having convenient locations. The service was average. The food wasn't good—and that's saying a lot, since I like pretty much anything I order. All of these restaurants were extremely lackluster, and yet … they were all packed.

The next few days, we decided to hop on TripAdvisor and see what else the island had to offer. We found a breakfast spot and a Mexican place that were in the hardest to find locations ever. Just when we thought we were lost, we turned several corners and walked down a few back alleys. And there they were! Both places were at the top of a TripAdvisor "Best of" list. Both offered amazing food and service. Both were highlights of our dining experience in Aruba! Both had TripAdvisor stickers and badges displayed proudly in every possible location in the building.

The manager of the Mexican place asked us to leave a review on TripAdvisor if we had a good experience. I was glad to do it—five stars all around. I overheard several people at the breakfast restaurant saying they'd found the place on TripAdvisor as well.

Both restaurants were busy. They were full of tourists. Without the TripAdvisor app, they'd undoubtedly be out of business in months due to their unfortunate locations.

Without the location advantage in a tourist market, you're pretty screwed. You need to take advantage of great reviews from past customers to give you visibility and credibility.

We didn't know anyone on the island, so first we asked the concierge at our hotel for advice about where to eat. We could tell the concierge was instructed to direct us only to the restaurants the hotel owned, which wasn't much help. The places with great locations were complacent; they didn't care. Customers were going to show up regardless of their efforts solely because of their proximity to the hotels.

If you are inside the United States, don't ignore TA either. The review volume isn't as high in non-tourist areas, but TripAdvisor is the go-to source for people looking for suggestions from people just like them.

Take advantage of this powerful resource to boost your business!

Chapter 4
GET SMART ABOUT
GETTING NOTICED

So now you know social media keeps you inside the fishbowl of your existing customers. It's an "opt-in" environment. You heard from customers in Chapter 1 that the most effective way to get new business, after word of mouth, is through online review platforms. That means primarily Google, Yelp, and TripAdvisor.

Don't believe me? How do you find a place to eat when you're on vacation in an unfamiliar place? When you get hungry, do you automatically open Facebook or Instagram and start mindlessly scrolling until you happen to come across a restaurant's post that happens to be in your area and happens to sound interesting?

Hell no.

Aside from asking a local or a trusted source for advice, you most likely go to one of two sources: Google or an online review app like Yelp or TripAdvisor. We Yanks rely pretty heavily on Yelp. Outside the United States, the go-to restaurant and bar app is TripAdvisor. These are both search-engine based and include ALL businesses; whether they joined in or not, they're all present.

Google and other search engines are open to anyone and everyone looking for your bar or restaurant without having to opt-in or even know you exist. This is the ocean of ALL consumers.

So the question is: How do you become a big fish in this ocean? How do you get noticed out there in the big wide world?

Well, let's start with what not to do.

DON'T Waste Money on the Perfect Website

Any website can give you a highlight reel of the business shown in the best possible light, but online reviews are brutally honest and mention the good with the bad. I read a statistic a few years back that said by the year 2020 websites will become obsolete. All of the info you need is already in the Google knowledge panel. This is the stuff that appears to the right side of a search and includes pretty much everything you're looking for.

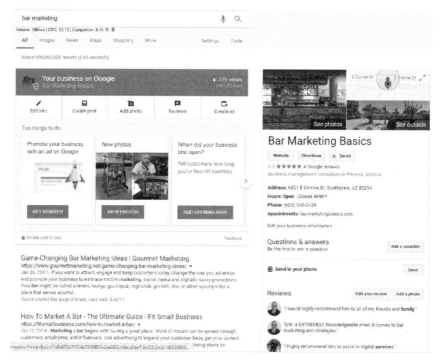

This panel lists contact info, pictures, hours of operation, reviews, directions, and everything a customer looking for a bar or restaurant would need in a search. Sure, they could click through to your website to see the extremely biased interpretation of your business based on what you think the public should see. But why would they do that when they have access to this unbiased source?

Don't get me wrong, as a web designer, I can honestly say you still need a website. Google still needs a source to pull the information from. And without a website, you are at a SERIOUS disadvantage. That being said, don't spend a lot of time and money on one. A basic website should run you no more than $1,500, unless you want serious bells and whistles. You don't need a Lambo here when a Ford Escort will get the job done.

Think of a website as a custom car you are having built.

Only *you* know EXACTLY what you want and how this car should look. But most people fail to specify exactly what they want. Let's stick with the custom car metaphor and take a look at how it plays out:

The customer tells their car designer, "I'd like you to build me a car. Here's the badge I want on the hood. Let me know when it's done." But this client fails to provide any parts or details, so the car builder is left to guess.

When the builder asks the client what he wants it to look like and how he'd like it to perform, the response is something like, "You're the car builder, not me. Show me what you think it should look and perform like. Build me three cars to pick from, and I'll let you know." Since building three cars will cost three times the price, they agree this is not an option. Nevertheless, it's almost always requested by the client!

So the builder takes months and months and produces a

great-looking car that gets great mileage, holds five people, and is affordably priced. When the client comes to the shop to take a look, he is instantly turned off. "Yeah, I was kinda expecting a truck. This thing needs to go off-road and have high ground clearance."

So the builder goes back to work and rebuilds the whole thing from the ground up. Months go by again, and he brings the client back in.

"Well, we're getting closer, but I was hoping it would be red. I also need navigation, backup cameras, Bluetooth, built-in Wi-Fi, and 12 airbags."

The builder explains those items were not discussed up front and will cost extra.

"But I assumed all that was just included! The last guy I got a quote from said it would have all of that. This is also taking way longer than I thought."

The builder goes back to the drawing board and tries to figure out a way to include all of this affordably and keep the peace. The truck needs to be stripped down again and rebuilt with all of the client's criteria included this time.

Meanwhile, the excited client is discussing his upcoming build with friends at cocktail parties and starts to get some input. A LOT of input.

It turns out there is another way to build this truck that doesn't require it to have high ground clearance—you just need to add better suspension to it instead.

"Yeah, I've changed my mind and need the truck built lower to the ground but with better suspension."

The builder agrees to make the changes, but that was not part of the original build, so it will cost you more since what you originally asked for has already been done.

"Now you're raising the price on me? This is ridiculous and taking WAY longer than we agreed to. This just isn't working out. I'm taking my build somewhere else!"

Had the client done the research first and figured out the options, or at least given the builder a chance to discuss the options, it would have gone something like this:

"I need a red truck built with all the bells and whistles with great suspension."

"Cool, here is the final price. Pick it up in a week!"

Seems simple, right? This is a constant battle I face with clients, and it's a story I've heard repeated constantly in the web design community. Here's another typical conversation designers run into with clients:

Designer: I'll need to get your content so I can build your website around it. You provide me the building blocks, and I'll arrange them so they look and flow great.

Client: Okay. I'll get it to you soon.

... Time goes by, and the designer receives no content ...

Client: Why does the website look so bare?

Designer: Because you never got me your content. Please send over everything you want to be included in your website. I can't arrange your building blocks in an attractive way without the blocks.

Client: Yes, I will. But why does it look so bare? It looks nothing like the theme we decided on.

Designer: Again, can I get your logo, hi-res images, any copy you want on there, your contact info, hours, please?

Client: Can't you just grab it off the existing website?

Designer: No, those images are way too small, and you explained you didn't want to use anything from your existing website. You also explained that nothing is accurate on that site.

... More time goes by ...

Client: Why is this taking so long?

Designer: Still need your content. I can't post something I don't have.

Client: Can't you just write the About Us section? I don't know why this should take so much time.

Designer: I'm a web designer, not a copywriter, not a mind-reader, not a photographer. Besides, I know nothing about your business, you do. Remember, I just take the information I'm given and make it look pretty and arrange it properly online. I can't build this thing without the raw materials.

Client: This is getting so frustrating. I just need this website done. Why does this take so long?

Designer: Since I can't pry any information from you, let's agree to go our separate ways. This isn't working out. And, no, I won't make your logo bigger.

I know this process very well because before I was the designer, I was this EXACT client! It's crazy how human nature works when it comes to website design, but I made the same mistakes when trying to get a site done years and years ago when I was the client and working in the real estate business. I'm just as guilty of this as everyone else.

One of the biggest running jokes in the web design business is "Could you make my logo bigger?" I'm not sure if this is an ego thing or what, but 100% of my clients bring this up the first time they see the rough draft. Have you ever looked at someone else's website and thought, "Great site, but that logo is so damn small!" It's probably never happened. Look at the big guys out there: Best Buy, Amazon, eBay. They all have really small logos. It makes sense. When the user is on your website, they know where they are; they don't need to be pounded over the head with this huge-ass logo!

So website building skills are awesome to possess because I can take an issue that's been a thorn in the side of my client for years and fix it in five minutes—once we pry the login info from the original designer, who they are no doubt on bad terms with ever since the miscommunication from the original build and way-longer-than-quoted time frames. This makes me look like a savior, and it makes the other guy look incompetent—even though chances are he didn't fix this issue because he never got paid his final check. This is a painfully predictable industry.

Don't create an idiot supermodel.

I cannot stress this enough.

Most restaurant and bar owners—hell, most website clients in general—will fixate on how the website LOOKS, paying little attention to anything else. With potential customers getting 99% of the info they need about your business from Google anyway, there is less and less of a need to actually click through to your site. Yes, you do need a website, but don't go overboard and don't focus on aesthetics. Your website is a marketing tool, not fine art. It's made for one thing and one thing only: to make you money.

Don't make your website the most amazing thing nobody has ever seen.

Just keep it simple. I design in WordPress exclusively. WordPress is easy to use, and it's totally free. It's not that other platforms like Wix or Squarespace are seriously flawed, but there's nothing at all wrong with WordPress and it'll do almost anything you need it to.

Do not reinvent this wheel; borrow someone else's. There are different features called "plug-ins" that you can add to your site to build on pretty much anything a restaurant would ever need. You can integrate things like Uber Eats or any delivery service, contact forms, calendars, slideshows, menus—all the extras.

WordPress and these other platforms are known as Content Management Systems (CMS). Meaning, you can log in and make your own edits after the fact without the need for the web designer. Any good designer will teach you how to use the site before rushing out of your life forever, but rarely does the client pay attention and actually learn it. Then when they need something, they'll inevitably call the designer (who won't answer) and get frustrated. LEARN. Pay attention to how to edit your site, I can promise you it will save aggravation and time in the long run.

Your restaurant's website shouldn't cost you more than $1,500. Do not pay an open-ended monthly fee for a website. Even if it sounds cheap. A "cheap" website could get pretty expensive if you're paying for it over the course of five years or more. A $99/mo. website will cost you $5,940 in five years. Another thing I hate is when companies charge for "hosting" your site. Even if it's super cheap, don't do this for several reasons. You can get your own hosting account for less than $150 per *year* through companies like GoDaddy. This way, you own the site, and you control your own content. If your content is on your web designer's hosting account, you don't really own it or have login info. Basically, you're his bitch if you want changes done. You're on his schedule, and his time will cost you.

I can say this because I am a web designer: web designers are some of the most unreliable people in existence. Before my time, there must have been a huge global meeting of web designers where they all made a pact. This pact runs deep into the web design community, and there are VERY few exceptions to the rule. The pact is simple: Whatever you do, do NOT respond when a client is trying to get a hold of you! Do NOT return emails until the fifth attempt. Do NOT ever listen to voicemails so your inbox is constantly full, preventing clients from leaving additional messages. And, for God's sake, ignore text messages at all costs!

Web designers are loyal to this pact; they rarely deviate from it. This was all agreed upon before I became a web designer, so I'm one of the few who didn't sign this pact.

DO Invest in SEO

Save yourself the time, money, and heartache you would have put into a worthless flashy website and, instead, invest it into getting found on an online search.

Getting found on Google makes you money.

This is a central aspect of what I do for my clients because it's not only hugely important but can be overwhelmingly complicated.

I'm talking about SEO. Search Engine Optimization. You should have a monthly budget for SEO. Take the money you're now not spending on stupid crap, like expensive hosting or monthly website builder fees, and put it all into search visibility.

I recently met with a potential client who had a custom-built WordPress website. It was nice but not spectacular. He hated it and wanted it redone. I told him there really wasn't anything wrong with it. Even though I could have made a quick buck, it didn't make sense to throw money into the site, so I advised him to leave it alone. His visibility was horrific. It was hard to find him in any sort of Google search. He then asked me to guess how much he had spent on the site. I said I hoped it wasn't something ridiculous like $5,000. Mentally, I was going through what I would have quoted him and landed around the $1,500 mark in my head.

He paid $10,000 and still couldn't be found on Google. Holy shit! Don't make this mistake!

Like I mentioned before, I give away all of my knowledge for free in this book because whether you have all the ingredients or not, time is not always on your side.

SEO is the only thing that the average person will not understand, nor would it interest them to learn. It can get insanely tech-nerdy, and it takes a special type of mind to have the attention span needed to learn the ropes. Keep in mind that, like everything online, SEO is constantly evolving, and the rules are continuously changing. It's like building the coolest Rally car ever and mastering the Rally track, only to find that the track has evolved into a Formula 1 track. If you refuse to update and adapt your car, you will slowly move into the irrelevant category and start racking up losses.

There is one rule of thumb that remains constant with ranking high in Google. <u>Don't half-ass it</u>. The more thorough you are, the better you'll rank. Hang on, let me put that in bold font.

The more thorough you are, the better you'll rank.

If you're the guy who fills out the bare minimum when creating your profile, you're half-assing it and you'll never rank toward the top. If there is a spot to upload your logo and ten pictures, don't just upload one. Upload all ten pictures. Don't have any good ones? Invest in getting professional photos taken. More on this later. For now, what you need to know is Google rewards people who put in the work and make an extra effort. Makes sense. So, if you can't do the work yourself, this is where you want to invest your money.

By the way, Yahoo and Bing are dead to me. When I say "search engines" I mean Google. It's the only one that matters anymore. You still want to be on Yahoo and Bing for the backlinks, but don't spend a lot of time there. What's a backlink? I'm glad you asked.

DO Focus on Backlinks

The more relevant the backlinks, the better.

Backlinks are links on other websites that connect back to yours. Any directories (lists of websites) or places you could potentially have a profile, you want to be there. The *quality* of the backlinks also plays a role. Meaning, if your restaurant has backlinks from your other business making custom belt buckles, it's pretty much worthless. I'm not going to get deep into backlinking because I'll lose most readers at that point. Reach out to me for this; it's one of the most effective services I offer my clients.

In order to rank well on Google, you have to have consistent and correct information online. If your business is called "Erik's Bar & Grill," don't have your name on a profile listed as "Erik's Bar & Grill—Scottsdale, AZ" even if you have multiple locations. This will throw off Google and hurt your ranking. The same thing goes for different contact information including phone numbers, hours of operations, etc. Separate locations of the same business should have completely different profiles with exactly the same name. The address field will let them know they are separate.

Multiple or duplicate listings is also a no-no. Let's say you have the bright idea of making a profile for your "restaurant" part of your business and double-dipping with an additional profile mentioning your "bar" aspect, this will do the exact opposite—it will *hurt* your search engine rankings. I was actually asked to do this way back in my country music bar days, and we reaped the rewards of this practice by being blackballed and removed from Google for a month or two. Don't try to cheat the system; Google has people working for them who are way, WAY smarter than you and I will ever be. If we've thought of it, they did first.

Now you know what Google is, here is what it isn't: Optimizing your search results in Google is not a magic wand. It doesn't happen overnight. It takes months and sometimes years to kick in. It's geared for long-term success and not a short-term spike in traffic. No marketing tactic will open the floodgates of people into your door no matter what that guy on Instagram said. Short of prime-time mainstream media attention with a great engaging story attached, marketing—including Google—is a slow, daily process. SEO will only make your brand more visible to potential customers. If your brand isn't appealing, it won't work nearly as well.

If you need help with anything Google My Business related, contact me personally (602-540-0128), or call Google at 844-491-9665.

Chapter 5
MAKE SOCIAL MEDIA WORK FOR YOU

It never fails. Every time I sit down with a prospective client and discuss marketing, they use the word "social media" interchangeably with the word "marketing." This is so ingrained in people's minds that even AFTER I sign on to take care of "reputation management and search engines," I'll get the call from their contact guy saying, "I hear you're our new social media guy. Great to meet you." I then have to explain I do not get into social media work at all. This is inevitably met with a long silence on their end. I'd love to ignore the subject of social media in this book, but most people think this way. So, instead of ignoring it, let's dive in.

I work in the ocean; I do not work in the fishbowl.

The game of social media is very hard to win and very easy to lose. It is opinion-based, not analytically based. It is not measurable. Its failure or success is rarely understood and almost always unproven. My opinions on social media as a marketer, by the way, are very unpopular. I am in the minority of people who think this way; yet, this is common sense to me.

When I say it's not measurable, I mean not successfully measurable. Sure, you could put a call to action on Facebook with something like, "Mention this post to your server to receive 20% off your tab." This would be measurable IF there were a button programmed in your POS system and then only IF the servers enter it correctly. This is the step that seems to fail 100% of the times I've tried this approach. It only works if all cylinders are firing correctly, which rarely happens in reality.

This book was written in 2018, and at this point in time, the only relevant social media platforms are Facebook and Instagram. So when I refer to "social media," I'm referring to these two platforms. Here is a real quick breakdown of which demographic uses which platform. Kids use Snapchat; if you have a bar, don't waste your time on this app. If you have a senior citizen demographic only, throw this book away now. The big picture is that Instagram skews younger, and Facebook skews older. Of the people I've polled, only about 0.7% use Twitter to find a restaurant. So, for our purposes, Twitter is dead to me as well.

I constantly hear about the "new Social Media hack that brought me 200% more profits in one week!" and other related bullshit. Just like Google, there is no shortcut in social media—with one exception. Paying for traffic. If you pay to sponsor posts or pay for other methods of expanding your reach, you can move people from the ocean into your fishbowl. Since we're on the subject, I don't recommend Google AdWords. It's got its purpose, but restaurants and bars are not included.

Here is my theory; again, it's pretty unpopular. Save your money. Don't pay a "social media guy" to post random crap all week long. Instead, assign a budget to pay a guy who is really good at targeted (paid) posts. This approach is WAY more measurable and astronomically more successful. Just keep in mind, this means you're paying the guy for his skills AND paying Facebook and Instagram for the reach. Do these once a week or every other week. Quality far outweighs quantity in today's online world.

Be the Show, Not the Commercial

Your marketing will start working when you stop *marketing to* people and start giving them exciting, enjoyable content that they WANT to engage with. Ask yourself what resonates with YOU and duplicate that. Do YOU like watching commercials on TV? My guess is hell no, you don't. Commercial time is when you get up, grab a drink, and check email until the "Show" comes back on. Ask yourself if you are a *Commercial* creator or a *Show* creator. Creating the *Show* is called *content marketing.*

Content marketing is 67% cheaper and three times more effective.

Creativity is free—remember that. Buying ineffective, poorly targeted Facebook ads and throwing money at a problem is just lazy. And expensive. Try to get out of the mind-set of looking at what everyone else is doing and duplicating it. Trust me, very few people have the answers. The number of businesses that do their homework and actually have original, engaging campaigns is staggeringly low. These days, people are actually copying/pasting terrible ideas and perpetuating the mundane, ineffective spammy approaches that haven't worked for a decade.

> Imagine a room full of people taking a test that none of them studied for. Everyone is copying off everyone else's paper, all producing different versions of the wrong answer. This is where online restaurant and bar marketing is today.

But, good news: with a great content marketing approach, it's EASY to rise above the mediocre masses and create an awesome brand!

Flyers Are Not Good Advertising

You remember my irritation with flyers from the beginning of this book. Here is my biggest gripe with most restaurants' social media approach: I'm a graphic designer who used to make a living by making flyers to be used online. Flyers are synonymous with advertising. Human nature states that people hate being advertised to. I hate it. Ask yourself: While scrolling through an endless sea of posts online, do I stop and read the ones that are obviously advertisements?

No. Flyers have become so irrelevant in people's minds that we subconsciously categorize them as having zero value within fractions of a second. Before we even see the words, our minds have dismissed them as meaningless to us! I realized I wasn't the only one who'd seen the light when I was in the business of sponsoring (paying for) Facebook posts for a dance club I worked for.

When you go to upload a flyer to advertise a certain event and sponsor the post, Facebook won't even allow you to do this. Facebook is a smart-as-hell platform built by smart people who value self-preservation. They KNOW posting flyers will be ignored by the public. Facebook's reputation would plummet if they allowed this, and they would lose money. You'd hear things like, "I keep sponsoring my posts with flyers, and I never get any response. Facebook doesn't work." They won't even allow more than 20% copy on a sponsored post, meaning flyers aren't allowed if you're paying. The post has to be a photograph with very little copy. The copy can, of course, go into the typed explanation at the top of the post. Most of these events have time, date, and venue details that should go here instead of the image. Facebook's success rate goes up *because of* censoring flyers. Everyone in the bar and dance club community was very annoyed when this rule came into effect years ago. Annoying? I think it's genius.

Using pictures or videos only is a far more successful approach with online posts.

Flyers are the most expensive, least successful form of advertising, yet many bar and restaurant marketers still fight for their right to fail this way.

Insanity.

Every successful person has two options for constant growth: pay a professional to do it for them, or learn how to do it themselves. Growing up broke, I opted for the latter. I learned web design, graphic design, and photography, among others.

Investing in professional photography for your business is not an option—it's absolutely required for online success. It's the building block that your entire online presence is based on. A high-quality SLR camera is what the professionals use. However, don't mistake everyone who happens to own an SLR for a good photographer. By the same token, downloading Photoshop doesn't make you a good graphic designer. If you'd like to learn the correct way to take a picture and how to use Photoshop then—by all means—maybe you can cut these costs. But there is a huge difference between a skilled professional behind the lens and some dude who happens to have a cool camera.

#Hashtags Are Worthless

Holy shit. Don't even get me started on hashtags! These have been the common sense thorn in my side since they made their way out of Twitter and into all other social platforms. Like I mentioned before, Twitter is irrelevant in this forum, so let's stay on the subject of Instagram and Facebook. Hashtags are a way to categorize things into common threads and related info. They made sense for Twitter, but just because 44" tall tires will help you off road doesn't mean you should put them on a Porsche.

Think of hashtags like this: They are basically keywords like you'd type into Google. So if you have a new product that is made specifically for BMWs, posting on Instagram with #bmw is a good tactic and actually works. If you have a national brand or a product that could potentially be purchased by someone across the country and shipped to them, then hashtag away! But this is not the case in our discussion of bars and restaurants. Let's take the example of #happyhour, which is used a TON in our industry's posts. Think of this as a Google search term—only without the geographic boundaries. So when you type "restaurants" into Google in your phone, it will pull up restaurants that are near you. A #happyhour hashtag search in social media will pull up every damn post from around the entire globe; it will show every instance of this same hashtag world-wide! Can you imagine using this method to find a restaurant in your area? It's pretty much impossible.

I get into this argument with people online probably way more than I should. I don't mean a random person; I'm talking about people in restaurant marketing forums who do this for a living! They almost always dig their heels in and argue the point, so I did a quick experiment. One of these people had just posted with #happyhour, so I did a quick hashtag search looking for her specific post on Instagram. I waded through posts from India, China, the United States, and Australia. I found a great picture posted by an awesome-looking restaurant in the Philippines, which I will never visit. What I DIDN'T find was her post from her restaurant here in Arizona, *which I was specifically looking for.*

Once again, my opinion on this matter is in the minority. All of these "social media experts" will tell you how much time they've invested in the correct use of hashtags. I've asked this question online and in several polls, and I've yet to have a single person find a single restaurant through a single hashtag. Ever.

Facebook is even more worthless of a platform to utilize hashtags than Instagram. I often get into arguments that go something like this: "Well, if it's not costing you any more money, what's the harm?" To me, the improper use of hashtags—and ESPECIALLY the overuse of hashtags—looks amateur and spammy. Input from real customers aligns with this idea. What's worse is that using more than seven hashtags in a post will often get it flagged as spam, which will greatly reduce your post's reach. Hashtags, in my opinion, are the resource most contributed to but least utilized in modern history. It's like having a warehouse full of millions and millions of driver's side front wheel bearings that only fit the '87 Saab 900 Turbo. Sounds impressive, but why?

If you're still in doubt, take it from the customer: According to my polling data, roughly 97% said they would not use hashtags to find a bar or restaurant to visit.

Enough said.

Paid Facebook Ads

I admit it. I used to say, "Paid Facebook ads don't work!" As long as you follow a few simple guidelines, they actually do work. Don't approach this like you would approach a free post on your restaurant or bar's business page. Free posts usually have little to no thought put into them, and the return is proportional. And since your wallet is on the line now that your FREE Facebook reach is choked down to less than 1% by Facebook algorithms, make it count.

Choose an Engaging Photo or Video

Choose something that will make people stop scrolling and say, "Whoa, that looks amazing!" Video will always get a better reach than any other format, so use it when you can. Attention spans these days are less than a second while scrolling social media. If your post doesn't grab your own attention in less than one second, move on until you find one that does. Pictures of your sexy female servers or bartenders ALWAYS work if done correctly. Keep them classy yet attractive.

Here is a weird anomaly that happened when I was polling the public and getting feedback on what type of post people find most appealing: People didn't admit to finding "attractive staff photos" (sexy girls) compelling. It came in almost dead last as a customer incentive. But according to the analytics, this type of photo gets the *most* likes almost every time. Kinda like how porn is a multibillion-dollar business, yet no one ever spends a dime on it.

Invest in Professional Photos and Video

Sound familiar? Yeah, I'm harping on this for a reason. You know what type of social media post gets a potential customer's attention? Great quality content. That's the tough part. Who cares *who* schedules it to post every other day? If you provide this person with 40–80 hi-res awesome looking pictures and videos of the food and the architecture of the building, 99% of the social media job is already done.

A professional photo shoot should cost you about $300–$500, and you can use these pictures for years. You can reuse them several times over the course of the year or more. And guess who the only person is that will actually see them multiple times? You. The public will never in a million years know that you are reposting content, nor will they care, as long as you don't go overboard.

Photo by J Martin Harris Photography

You can use professional photos for more than this, though. Social media is only the beginning. Use your photos and video to build a website, for video content, on TV screens. Basically, anywhere you market your business, you can use professional photos and video clips.

Have you ever seen a professional TV commercial shot with an old cell phone? Hell no. They all use state-of-the-art equipment to paint their product in the best possible light. They make these commercials as entertaining and visually stimulating as possible. You've built the Ferrari of restaurants, but then show it to the world via crayon drawings because you figured you didn't need to worry about it or assumed it would be too expensive. Crap in, crap out.

Choose Your Target Carefully

Don't fall into the trap of choosing "people who like your page and their friends" when it comes to targeting posts. This sounds like a no-brainer, but remember we're trying to bring in NEW people here. If the people who have already heard of you and follow you on Facebook see your ads, it's most likely nothing new to them; you're paying for meaningless reach. Choose your demographics correctly. Do not cast too wide a net. Bigger numbers do not necessarily equal more people in the door. The quality of your customers is WAY more valuable than quantity when it comes to paid Facebook and Instagram ads for restaurants.

To be totally honest, paid posts are not my area of expertise, but like I mentioned in previous chapters, seek out someone who specializes in this for bars and restaurants and trust their experience. Nick Fosberg is a great resource for this. Visit Nick's website at *https://barrestaurantsuccess.com*.

Chapter 6
PAY ATTENTION TO NEW TECHNOLOGY

You know those guys who call all day and ask if the owner is in? Or that uncomfortable-looking suited-up guy who stops in and asks for the manager on duty? Your immediate reaction is, *Shit, how can I hide from this guy without him noticing me?* The go-to excuse is … you guessed, it "Tell him I'm in a meeting right now." Managers—and humans, in general—do almost everything they can to avoid salespeople.

I'm exactly the opposite.

I've been on both sides of the equation for years. I'll admit I used to avoid these people like the plague. When I was on the other side of the equation walking into bars cold to introduce myself, I realized how bad it had gotten. Every salesperson who came before me was a real-life version of spam. But I had something of value they needed to see! Yeah, everyone thinks that. But I actually did, and I've made a pretty good living from it.

So I changed my tactics. When I worked at corporate offices more recently, I'd take a meeting with every one of these guys who had the balls to walk in the door and ask for one. It often caught them off guard when I'd say, "Yep, I have time right now. Let's talk!"

Some of the best pieces of software I've ever seen came from this.

Now when someone finds me online and wants to pitch me, my answer is ALWAYS yes. I will listen to anyone who has something of value, or who at least thinks they do. Some people are just regurgitating social media garbage, but this is actually rare. How can you learn or discover new ways to make money for your business if you won't even give salespeople a simple meeting? I recommend more money in your pocket over less money 100% of the time. If you're busy, then schedule a time to hear these people out. Or keep reading and I'll give you the best of what I found by taking the meetings.

System Social (systemsocial.com)

This is an online platform that allows you to write and send a social media post with one click to your entire staff. With one more click on their end, it will post on their personal social media accounts on the restaurant's behalf. The best part is they have analytics built in so you can see which of your staff members are participating and which are not. Kindergarten gold-star boards are a thing of the past. Since your restaurant's Facebook page is now close to worthless, you can leverage your staff's profiles, which still yield quite a bit of reach.

Enplug (enplug.com) and Upshow (upshow.tv)

These two platforms are similar in that they let you display flyers and promotions— and even your customers' Instagram posts—on your in-house TV screens. These are great for music venues that have upcoming shows or other events you'd like your in-house captive audience to know about. The social media integration part is cool and works in certain environments, but not necessarily others. They also allow you to display your own restaurant or bar's social media content on these screens. At the time I tested these, they both had flaws. For example, if you display your own social media post about a UFC fight, the system has no way to know when that fight has already happened and will unknowingly display an expired event. This is, however, a rare problem. It's worth your time to at least explore these two platforms. As opposed to flyer content on social media, in-house flyer content works much better. Check out their websites for more info.

Zenreach (zenreach.com) and Cogobuzz (cogo. buzz) WiFi Marketing Systems

If you have an open, unlocked WiFi network for your customers to log into, that's cool and all, but if you're not benefiting from this, you're missing out on the opportunity to market to your WiFi users. Zenreach and Cogobuzz are two platforms that allow you to do just that.

While they both allow you to capture the customer's email or social media account, Cogobuzz goes a step further by adding a phone number capture and a text message option. I like that extra feature. With Cogobuzz, it goes something like this: A customer logs into the WiFi and is prompted to enter their phone number before being granted online access. The system will immediately send them a welcome text thanking them for connecting. This is your chance to mention an upcoming event, a drink special, or whatever you'd like to mention. When they come back through the door "X" number of times later—a number you get to determine—the platform will send them a "Welcome back" message. You guessed it—another opportunity to get a message in front of the customer while they're in your place.

Zenreach uses a cool system they call "smart emails," which sends out emails based on landmarks. You can customize messages to appeal to the following people: the first-time customer, the repeat customer, the loyal customer, and the lost customer. You can also send an invite for a customer's upcoming birthday. Each of these emails goes out one by one as needed, so they are a lot less likely to get filtered into spam or filed under Gmail's "promotional" tab. I use the first-time customer email as a reputation-management tool, asking customers, "How did we do?" The customer can then answer with 1–5 stars. Any negative experiences hopefully get brought up at this point, so we have the opportunity to fix the issue before it ends up on Yelp.

Both of these platforms offer more functionality, but these are the basics. They are easy to set up, and the analytics are great. I use one of these for almost all of my clients. Last time I checked, both of these were around $200 a month or less.

Localfluence (localfluence.com)

As in "Local Influence." Once you get past the name, this company has a really cool idea. We now know that social media posts from real people, not businesses, carry the most weight. This platform provides an amazing blend of social media and word of mouth. Localfluence will send Instagram "influencers" in the door of your business to eat your food and post real, organic photos to their own Instagram account. They'll tell their friends and family about your business. The posts look like genuine posts with the influencer telling the world about this cool new spot they discovered! It works because it isn't salesey and doesn't come off as being promotional. THIS is virtual word of mouth at its best.

In return, the business gives the reviewer something of value, usually a voucher for $15 in credit, a free entrée, or something to that effect. It has to be something substantial for the influencer to come in.

Localfluence also takes a small fee, but it's usually around 8–10 bucks a person. You only pay for the people who actually post on social media. It gets better: the influencers are also asked to write a 5-star review on the review platform of their choice with an honest review of their experience. Of course, if the experience was negative, they're asked to keep it internal; they handle it with management themselves so the bad review never goes public. This is a very simplistic service— so simple it's brilliant.

Table Tent Options

Now you can up your table tent marketing game with custom laser-cut metal table tents. If you're still rockin' the acrylic table tents you got from your liquor distributor then you really need to take a closer look at improving your customer experience.

Send a strong message with a custom-made metal tent with your logo burned into the sides. Use multiple pages on these to increase the marketing value, and give the customer as much info as possible. Last time I checked, these go for around $15 each, so the investment is pretty minimal. Check these out at rpmmetal.com.

If you want to go high-tech, you can use a mini-screen/phone charger table topper from companies like One Stone (useonestone.com). These will display your upcoming promotions, happy hour specials, or whatever else you want, and it gives customers a great place to charge their phones. These tiny double-sided screens are used on your tables or bar top, within close view of your captive audience. A full charge lasts about a day or two, so they do require charging once drained.

Chapter 7
THE BUSINESS OWNER'S BEST PRACTICES

YOU are your brand. You've heard of Gordon Ramsay and Bobby Flay for a reason. Cash in on being the face of your business. Being a "behind the scenes" owner or manager is okay, but if you really want to tap into the value, be the face of your business. Leverage social media through your personal profile instead of a business page. When your customer base knows you're PASSIONATE about your business instead of a guy wanting to make a buck, business will start to roll in. People love authenticity, honesty, and passion.

Be Accessible

Unless you are a hands-off owner and you have the luxury of not being bothered, answer your damn phone! Are you in the habit of not answering your phone or being generally unreachable? STOP IT. It's costing you business! Being in the habit of letting your calls go to voicemail is also costing you time. Instead of answering the phone and answering questions that usually take a minute or so, you now have a growing list of voicemails you need to sift through that eat up your day. You'll be surprised how much of your day gets freed up by NOT HAVING voicemails in the first place. No, you're *not* too busy to answer your phone. You're too busy *because* you don't answer it.

People seem to be scared to death to publish their cell number anywhere online. I say publish away! My cell number is posted all over review sites like Yelp for unhappy people to be able to reach out to me so I can defuse a tense situation, but you know what also happens? Pissed off people just about to write a shitty Yelp review will see my number on someone else's review and call me first. Guess what? I just defused a situation without it ever getting into the dreaded 1-star Yelp territory by simply providing a cell number. (P.S., my cell number is 602-540-0128.)

Don't Second-Guess the Pros You Hired

You hired the right people to run your business. You interviewed dozens of people and found just the right guys to help you operate. You trust them to promote, organize, and fill your bar. Then you question their plans and direction? If they have a record of success then back off, do what you do best, and let them do the same. Spend a bit more money or time to hire the RIGHT person so you don't have to second-guess their decisions in the first place. This will always be money well spent.

Choose Your Chef Wisely

The biggest complaints that deter people from returning are poor service and poor food. I asked the public: If you could only have one of the following, which would you choose? Average service but awesome food OR average food but awesome service. A whopping 75% said they prefer the awesome food and average service. So if your kitchen isn't on point, you're eventually gonna get chopped.

Similarly, I asked what the biggest deal breaker would be for not returning. Once again, bad food took the top spot at 36%. Poor service was directly below it with 30%. Other factors included a dirty facility, bad atmosphere, overpriced menu, long waits to be seated, too far away, and scarce parking. When this question was asked in reverse, the answers were more or less the same. When I asked what factor would make customers return to a bar or restaurant the MOST, "great food" took the lead at 45%, followed by "great service" at 24%.

The regular (return) customer is, of course, the cheapest to get in the door, plus he or she is hopefully telling others how cool your restaurant is, so they'll become little brand ambassadors as well. The frequency of visits is where the magic is. When I asked customers what types of places they visit most frequently, the place with the "best food regardless of the concept" once again took the top spot with 32%. Small family-owned businesses were also at the top. Chain restaurants and high-end or trendier places brought up the rear. These trendy types of places are usually reserved for special occasions.

We all know it costs vastly less to cultivate a one-time customer into a repeat customer, so keep this bit of human nature in mind. When I asked people what their dining and drinking habits were in their familiar hometown areas, 44% said they usually visit the same bar and restaurants repeatedly. This shows you the power of providing a great customer experience and how the experience can trigger a snowball effect either in a positive direction or a negative one. The happy customer costs a lot less to get back in the door for another visit. AND these customers use their voice to multiply your marketing efforts, which is also the most trusted and effective method.

Make Your Return Customers Happy

How do you keep returning customers happy? The customer experience trumps everything. The entire point of the great food, nice presentation, friendly staff, millions of dollars put into architecture and environment all boils down to one thing: *the customer experience.* A poor customer experience will shut your business down quickly. Enough negative experiences over a long enough timeline doom your business to fail. This is not an opinion. Jon Taffer calls these *reactions*; I prefer the term *experience.* We are not in the restaurant and bar business, we're ALL in the *people business.* People can be irrational pricks sometimes, and when you add alcohol to a person who's already an asshole sober, you have a recipe for a true challenge. Success comes from finding ways to overcome these challenges. If it were easy, everyone would do it.

Those people who open a restaurant or bar because they think it'll be fun are staring down the barrel of a loaded cannon without even knowing it. "I mean, how hard could it be, right?" These people are adorable. There's nothing wrong with wanting a challenge, but 99% of the time the "bar owner" that hasn't been in the trenches before has no idea what kind of shit storm he or she just signed up for. If this is you, I applaud you for having the balls to do it, just know that this business will chew you up and spit you out if you aren't prepared. Whether you have the experience under your belt or not, the customer experience is absolutely crucial to success. This may sound like common sense, but it's overlooked every day, in every restaurant, in every city. Running a restaurant is fucking TOUGH! It's long, thankless hours and high stress 24 hours a day.

Keep Your Staff on Their Toes

You own or manage the place for a reason—you did the work to make it happen. Getting your staff to think like you is another challenge altogether. Your staff is most likely young, and this is probably not going to be their choice of career. It's a stepping stone to get where they really want to be. Your business to them is a necessary inconvenience in life.

I'm constantly working on my weaknesses, and public speaking is definitely one of them. So I decided to kill two birds with one stone and improve on this. I began speaking to the staff of my clients and trying to change their mind-set. It's really nothing they haven't heard before from their bosses, but when it's delivered by a third party, they tend to pay attention and absorb the information. Kinda like how your parents told you to quit playing in the street because it's dangerous and you blew them off until you got yelled at by the guy who almost hit you with his car; shit starts to sink in all of a sudden.

This is the speech I give to bar and restaurant staffs. Feel free to rip this off and adapt it to your own purposes. This will have a positive effect on your customer's experience if delivered correctly; I have no doubt of that.

I arrange an all-hands-on, front-of-house meeting. I start by greeting the servers, bartenders, and FOH staff. Then I ask them to turn off their phones and put them away. I start with a brief summary of my background in the trenches that you read in the introduction. After that, it goes a little something like this:

> *I am here for you people, not the owner. This is not about your boss's wallet; this is about yours. I'm here to make YOU more money, plain and simple.*

> *Two-thirds of the new customers who come in your door are from word of mouth. As a marketing expert, I can only really affect 33% of the people who walk in this door. The rest is up to you. You all are responsible for influencing word of mouth. Will you influence it positively or negatively? Every table and every guest will be*

influenced by you directly. Future business hinges on how you influence the customer.

I have a term I love that applies to everyone in every line of work, in everyone's personal life, every single day.

"RUTHLESSLY SELF-SERVING."

Everything you do every day should serve you. Everything you do should be to improve and better yourself. Being ruthlessly self-serving will increase your bank account 100% of the time. Do not confuse this with being selfish. Helping others feels good; helping others serves YOU. When you quit arguing with coworkers and start having their back instead, this will serve YOU.

Will rolling out of bed with ten minutes to get to work and showing up with your hair and makeup looking like you've been up all night partying help your tips? This does NOT serve you.

Look the part physically, and feel the part mentally before every shift. Your wallet will thank you. Be prepared. Every. Single. Shift.

Providing a great customer experience is painfully simple, but it requires a bit of thought. Start to take a mental tally of a few things:

Remember the NAME.

Remember the DRINK.

Remember the CONVERSATION.

If you remember these three things—not only with the regulars but with the customers who have been in only once before—your tips WILL increase. If a customer came in the door one time a few weeks ago and on his second visit you remember his drink, he's pretty impressed, right? Your tips go up because you took a small interest in this person and made a mental note of what he ordered.

Now if you ask people's names and REMEMBER them, do you think your tip will increase even more upon their next visit? Hell yes.

Let's take it a bit further. If you are in the position of having the opportunity to make small talk with people, remember the conversation. Picture this: You are talking with a customer, and he mentions briefly that his wife is going into the hospital for an unknown symptom. You wish him luck and that's it. Now when he comes back through the door a month later and you ask how his wife is doing with the hospital visit, he will undoubtedly be impressed. Your tip will absolutely go up!

When you remember all three consistently, you are now making bank compared to your previous self! Picture this: **"Hey, John. Great to see you again! Vodka tonic? How did everything go with your wife? I hope the symptoms ended up being nothing."** *You just blew that guy's mind. You are now his go-to bartender or server. He is now a regular customer who asks to be seated in your section. Be interested and involved. Look your best. Don't do it for them, do it for YOU. Your following will increase. Your bank account will go up. And this didn't require one more second of work in your day than you work right now.*

Stay off the phone! I'm going to say it again because this is the biggest factor in modern life that is separating you from making more money. Stay off the damn phone! I know some people have genuine addictions to their phones, so if this is you, keep it in the back of house and not in your pocket. When a customer sees you typing on the phone, it sends a very clear message: "My personal life is more important than you."

I work in reputation management for bars and restaurants, and this is consistently at the top of the list of customer complaints. If you manage social media for the restaurant on your phone, cool! Do it in the back of the house or before your shift. There is absolutely zero reason why you have to be on the phone within sight of a customer.

You have one of the only job descriptions that includes the ability to give yourself a raise at any time you choose.

When you follow these steps and start to be ruthlessly self-serving, your tips WILL go up. Probably starting the minute you decide to switch your thinking. Then over the course of the next week. Then the next month. And so on. Your boss does not have this power. The owner of the company does not have this power. You do, so use it! Want more money per shift without working one minute longer than you do now? Become ruthlessly self-serving.

People don't buy from businesses—they buy from people. Your regulars come to your place to see you. Sure, you may have great burgers too, but everybody has a great burger. No one is going to do business with someone they don't like or with someone they think doesn't like them. Sometimes you gotta act—I get it. When I was bartending, some of my regulars were a bit abrasive, but as far as they knew, I was their best friend inside those walls. Your job is to turn a one-time customer into a regular, so ACT the part. Some of the best bartenders in history are also great actors.

Don't "follow policy" because those are the rules; follow them because there's a very good chance they will serve YOU. Policies are in place to protect the business, which is nothing more than an outlet for you to make money. I'm almost positive your bosses are self-serving; they just want you to join them.

Post your shifts and upcoming events on your social media accounts. Not because you're required to do it. Don't do it because it's the policy. Do it because it will serve YOU. Your friends and followers will stop in to see you because of this. And guess what? There's a really good chance they're going to leave a tip.

Toxic people will ruin this environment. The people who confuse "self-serving" with "selfish." The ones who are only concerned about themselves and won't help out a coworker. The ones who won't pick up a shift when needed, or won't have someone's back. These are the people who will NOT succeed. Don't be this guy, and everyone will win. Never allow this to be you.

How you do one thing is how you do all things.

Apply this mind-set to everything in your life. I know there's a very, very good chance you're not going to be in this line of work for the rest of your life. At least not your current job description. When you start thinking with a ruthlessly self-serving mind-set, the world opens up for you. Apply this to your personal life. Apply this to your kids. Hell, apply this to your ex that you can't stand, and watch their attitude toward you change as well. Helping others can and will serve you. Huge jumps in personal growth happen when you start putting yourself first by helping people.

So remember when you clock in next time, you're not working for this restaurant or bar. You're working for YOU. You are your own little independent contractor who can very much affect the amount of money you take home on your very next shift. Don't be the person that complains about being broke yet does nothing to fix it.

You are just as responsible for bringing people in the door as your boss's marketing efforts, and believe it or not, you're waaaaaaaay more effective at it. Remember: you bring two-thirds of the people back through those doors. I could never do that—even with a decade of marketing experience.

There are a ton of options to eat and drink out there. Being better than all of them is EASY. Best of all, it doesn't require a single change to your current schedule or require you to work one minute more. Choose to be successful, and help others by being ruthlessly self-serving."

The Single Best Bartender I've Ever Experienced

I also include the following few stories in the talk I do for the staff as a way to illustrate the power of great customer service.

I briefly lived in Las Vegas, and the old rule holds true: if you live in Vegas, you do everything possible to avoid going to the Strip. I was no exception. Except when friends would come to town—then I didn't have a choice. We'd hit the Strip, and I'd show them around. One of my go-to bars was Carnival Court, which most people know as the outdoor circle bar between the Linq and Harrah's right on the Strip. This is a flair bar, which employs some of the best flair bartenders in the world. These guys are the ones who win the Legends of Bartending series all the time. To put it simply, they are the best of the best.

I'd bring friends to this place, and the bartenders always delivered. They would constantly get $20, $50, $100 tips. We knew this because they would make a huge deal about it, yell it out, and wet the bill and stick it to their foreheads. The customer felt VERY appreciated because of this. The rest of the people couldn't help but notice the $50 bill stuck to the guy's face, so they would up their tipping game as well. It was very contagious. Just like bringing sizzling fajitas through a crowded restaurant is a sure way to increase fajita sales.

My drink at the time was a Jack & Coke. I ordered a few times from several of the bartenders there over the course of a few months. Rene, Mig, and Christian all took orders from me, but none of them knew me. Aside from their names, I didn't know them either. I never had a conversation with any of them that lasted more than a brief 30 seconds of entertainment. These guys were attentive and professional yet wildly entertaining at the same time.

I moved out of Vegas after my brief stint in Nevada to Arizona, and I focused on work. I really wasn't doing much at this time. Years went by, and I finally got a chance for a weekend vacation. When you live in the Phoenix valley, you vacation in three areas of the country almost exclusively. San Diego, Rocky Point Mexico, and Vegas. For this one, we chose Vegas. And of course, we put Carnival Court on the list. We show up, and I see the usual suspects working the bar. Again, they don't have any idea who the hell I am. I'm one of the gazillions of tourists they make drinks for on a daily basis.

We end up getting to the front of the bar and ordering from a dude named Christian. He's the guy with the ponytail who served me before, years ago, but we haven't had a conversation since that time. He looks at me with a bit of a concentrated stare. He then points at me and says, "Jack & Coke, right?" "Holy shit, yes!" I said. He asked me about details he remembered from my last visit, which I barely remembered myself. He then asked my name. Now I know that it was to put in the mental Rolodex for next time, which he did not have the first time around.

My tab between my friends and myself was $48. I paid him a fifty and a hundred and told him to keep it. Of course, the excitement went way up. He wet the bill and pasted it to his forehead. "One-hundred-dollar tip!" he yelled out over the megaphone. The crowd went wild, and his tips started rolling in from there—all about the same denomination. In the next hour or so we were there, I counted about $1,500 going into his tip jar. This was ALL made possible and ignited by one thing: remembering some random guy's drink. This is how the best in the world roll.

Lessons I Learned from Baristas

One of the other monuments of outstanding experiences is Dutch Bros. coffee. Now, everyone has a bad day. No one can be "on" 100% of the time. Except for Dutch Bros. employees. These youngsters are not yet old enough to drink and really don't have many life experiences, yet they provide the best customer service of all time. Every. Damn. Time.

These people are taking orders from our pre-caffeinated asses every morning and pulling it off beautifully. They smile every time. They're happy every time. They ask, "How's your day going?" *every damn time.* If someone could bottle that, they'd be a millionaire. Okay, the Dutch Bros. owners are almost certainly millionaires. They were on Undercover Boss, and they looked like they were pretty comfortable in life.

Starbucks can't pull this off. Starbucks employees are the exact same demographic making the exact same money, if not more. Starbucks employees are miserable the majority of the time. Maybe they've improved recently, but I wouldn't know because I haven't been there since I started going to Dutch Bros. They both sell the same … exact … shit. Anyone can sell a cup of coffee, and the options are all pretty much identical.

Anyone can sell a Jack & Coke, but only the best can sell one for $100.

What a Cracked Cell Phone Screen Tells You

Is your cell phone screen currently cracked or, better yet, shattered beyond readability? If it cracked a few days ago and you'll get it fixed tomorrow then you get a pass. I'm talking about the people who constantly have a shattered cell phone screen. When the biggest, baddest new phone comes out, certain people line up for something they can't afford and don't need and redirect the rent check to that new shiny phone, only to be dropped and shattered again the next day. You know the guy or girl who is a victim of this. Over the years, I've done quite a bit of completely unscientific observational research. In my "research," I've noticed one consistently recurring theme: these cracked-phone people lead lives of chaos and are usually quite a mess.

The majority of people in the nightclub business and especially the young ladies in the "professional dancer" line of work all have shattered phone screens. I'll go out on a limb to say damn near every one of them, since I've made it a point to notice, all possess this same character trait. It's the same person who is always calling in "sick." The same person who always has a story of what a mess their life is. The same person who leads a life of total chaos and confusion—and excuses. The same person who is a professional victim. They almost all have this telltale sign.

Where am I going with this? Call it a cautionary tale or a way to know what you're getting into when putting your number into their phone. During a job interview, chances are they will plop their phone down on the table. Take mental notes. If that phone is shattered, you can almost guarantee chaos will follow.

If your current employee is behind the bar texting through the barely readable spider-webbed screen of their phone, you know what to do. I hope this helps.

LAST CALL

If you got anything out of this book, it should be that "experts" most likely don't know what they claim to know and have their own wallet in their best interests, not yours. Do your research and give people with new ideas a chance. This book was written in 2018, so in a few years tops, it too will probably be obsolete. Technology moves fast and is constantly evolving. What's true today may not be true tomorrow.

I know I sound like a self-defeating marketing expert who is telling you marketing doesn't work. Well, yeah, that's kinda true. It's more bullshit than reality. I wrote this book because the tidal wave of people trying to sell you their snake oil is overwhelming when you're trying to simply learn how to increase guest counts. I'd rather be the guy that helps you avoid the path of useless crap. I'm your bullshit detector. I'd rather make a friend than a buck. I'd rather have you buy me a drink than pay me for this book. I wrote this book in three days, ending on my 47th birthday. Not because I'm a good writer but because it comes easy when this is all you think about for a decade.

Like I mentioned, I have no problem giving away every bit of knowledge I have. I don't have any "big secrets" or "keys to unlocking millions." Do the work, do your research, and reap the rewards. Plain and simple. I do not work in the opinion-based, unproven world inside the fishbowl of social media. I choose to work in the measurable, quantifiable ocean of which ALL consumers are members.

You can hire me and Bar Marketing Basics to get you found easier on Google and improve your online reputation, but now you also have the tools to do it yourself. My fees max out under $400 per month for my clients, so if you don't have the time to do all of this yourself, please reach out to me. I'd love to talk.

The good news is, if you'd rather take this on yourself, you can. You are way more equipped now than you were before reading this book.

Best of luck to you! Who knows? Maybe we'll see each other in Vegas sometime. I'll be the guy at Carnival Court with the Jack & Coke.

—Erik Shellenberger

Marketing Skeptic

THANK YOU!

Thank you for reading this book! I wouldn't be where I am today without business owners like you taking an interest in making their bar or restaurant the best it can be. I hope you have more tools to run a successful place now. This book is not a sales tool but meant to provide some free value from the decade of experience I have in this industry. That said, if you'd like to continue to grow your business, I invite you to reach out to me directly. I focus on getting my clients found on Google and Reputation Management almost exclusively, but I'd be glad to take a look at your entire business to identify strengths and scout out weaknesses that can be improved. My website barmarketingbasics.com is constantly evolving, and new video blogs are added weekly. If you'd like to discuss how I can help your business, reach out to me at 602-540-0128 or erik@barmarketingbasics.com. Find me on Facebook or Instagram at @erikshellenberger.

FREE BONUS FOR YOU!

Now that we're complete, I have a free bonus to offer you.

In addition to the information already provided in this book, I would like to show you a scan of your business to see how well you rank in Google and what can be done to improve this ranking.

To receive your free scan, go to my website at barmarketingbasics.com and fill out the from titled "How does YOUR online visibility rank?"

Submitting a scan request up will also notify you of any pending book releases or updated content. By subscribing you will be first in line for exclusive deals and future book giveaways.

Immediately after signing up you'll be sent an email with access to this report.

—Erik Shellenberger

BEFORE YOU GO...

Do you want more?

Subscribe to my Youtube channel to receive more free tips and trick for improving guest counts and driving business.

What are you waiting for?

Subscribe now: youtube.com/ErikShellenberger

Thank you so much for choosing to be on this journey with me. I am glad that you stopped by.

Please do not hesitate to connect with me if you have any questions come up about this book, or if you just want some free advice.

I would be happy to hear from you and I enjoy connecting with readers.

Thanks again,

—Erik Shellenberger

A QUICK FAVOR PLEASE?

Before you go can I ask you for a quick favor?

Good, I knew I could count on you.

Would you please leave this book a review on Amazon?

Reviews are very important for authors, as they help us sell more books. This will in turn enable me to write more books for you.

Please take a quick minute to go to Amazon and leave this book an honest review. I promise it doesn't take very long, but it can help this book reach more readers just like you.

Thank you for reading, and thank you so much for being part of the journey.

—Erik Shellenberger

ABOUT THE AUTHOR

Erik Shellenberger has been in the restaurant and bar industry since he was 13 years old and worked for his mother in the food and beverage department at a Utah ski resort. Since then, he has held every position from dishwasher to bartender to marketing director and everything in between. With a decade of corporate marketing experience, he has gone from student to teacher and now runs Bar Marketing Basics (barmarketingbasics.com). He has quickly grown his client base, expanding beyond his hometown of Scottsdale, Arizona, to connect with clients across the nation, as far away as the East Coast.

Made in the USA
Columbia, SC
05 February 2020